故宮珍寶

責任編輯：許愛仙
封面題字：楊　新
封面設計：鄭志標
裝幀設計：徐小燕
日文翻譯：殷宏川
英文翻譯：王逢鑌
　　　　　程　玲

出　　版	紫禁城出版社
制版印刷	河北新華印刷一廠
發　　行	新華書店北京發行所
開　　本	12 開　889×1194mm　印張　5.5
版　　次	1995 年 3 月第一版第一次印刷
書　　號	ISBN7-80047-193-4/J・86

004000

目　　錄

目　　次

CONTENT

前　言

　　故宮博物院，不但以它巍峨壯麗的宮殿建築吸引着千百萬中外觀眾，同時也以它豐富多彩的古代文化藝術品珍藏而聞名世界。爲了幫助廣大觀眾瞭解這座古老的東方文化藝術寶庫，我們曾編輯出版了《紫禁城》圖册，重點介紹了故宮的宮殿建築。現在編輯出版的《故宮珍寶》，則重點介紹它的珍藏。

　　歷代以來，皇室對於文化藝術品及各種奇珍異寶，蒐集不遺餘力，明、清尤盛。故宮博物院是在明、清兩代皇宮基礎上建立起來的，主要繼承了這兩代皇室的收藏。1924 年末代皇帝溥儀被逐出宮廷以後，清室善後委員會曾對當時宮內文物進行了清點登記，總計有 117 萬餘件。抗日戰爭時期，爲了保護這批珍貴文物不致遭到戰火的燬滅，曾將部份文物裝箱疏散到大後方。日本投降後，除少部份運回北京本院外，其中最精華的部份計 2972 箱於 1949 年被運往臺灣，餘下 2211 箱仍寄存在南京庫房。

　　中華人民共和國成立後，故宮博物院對原清宮舊藏文物再次進行了整理登記，計有 78 萬餘件。作爲國家博物館，故宮博物院同時肩負有蒐集保存保護中華民族珍貴文化遺產的責任，因此，通過收購、接受捐贈等渠道，新入藏的文物有二十幾萬件。到目前爲止，現藏北京本院的文物總數達一佰餘萬件。

　　故宮博物院所收藏的文物，除了數量驚人之外，在內容和質量上也是世人所矚目的。從歷史的發展講，遠到原始社會新、舊石器時代，歷商、周、秦、漢，經隋、唐、五代、兩宋，而至元、明、清和近現代，都有代表性文物收藏。如果將這些文物係列性展示，那將是中華民族數千年文化藝術發展歷史的縮影。從文物門類來説，有陶瓷、玉器、青銅、碑石、印璽、法書、名畫、漆器、琺瑯、織綉、金銀器、各種寶石製品、竹木牙骨雕刻、家具等等，真是琳瑯滿目，美不勝收，這是我們國家一筆最可寶貴的文化藝術遺產。

　　如此數量眾多、歷史久遠、豐富多彩的文化藝術品珍藏，要想全部出版介紹出來，幾乎是不可能的。這裏編輯出版的《故宮珍寶》，那真正是萬裏挑一。我們的目的，主要不在於研究歷史文物，祇是想通過它，幫助參觀遊覽者初步瞭解一下，故宮博物院究竟收藏了一些甚麼，而能留下一個深刻印象。當然，這本册子容納雖小，但它所選用的品種門類很多，歷史的跨度也很大，代表性也很強，我想這個目的是能達到的。

　　中華民族是一個歷史悠久的偉大民族，有着無窮的智慧和力量，具有豐富的想象力和創造才華，對未來充滿着憧憬和信心，我想每一個到故宮來參觀的遊覽者，通過對宮殿建築的欣賞和對它收藏的文化藝術珍品的瞭解，都會有這樣深切的體會。中華民族所創造的歷史文化財富，也是世界人民的寶貴財產。故宮博物院已經被聯合國科教文組織列爲世界文化遺產保護單位。願人們都來關心、愛護、保衛好這座東方文化藝術寶庫。

故宮博物院副院長　楊新

はじめに

　故宮博物院はその雄大で、壮麗な宮殿建築で国内外の観光客を引き付けているばかりでなく、豊富多彩な古代文化芸術品を収蔵していることでも世界にその名を知られている。多くの皆様にこの古い東方文化芸術の宝庫を知ってもらうために、私達は、かつて『紫禁城』という図録を出版して、故宮の宮殿建築に重点をおいて紹介したことがあるが、今回出版の『故宮珍宝』では主にその収蔵品を紹介する。

　歴代の皇室は、文化芸術品や各種珍宝の収集に尽力してきたが、とくに、明時代と清時代が最も盛んであった。現在の故宮博物院は明、清両時代の皇宮をもとにして造られ、主にこの二つの時代の収蔵品を継承している。1942年,最後の皇帝溥儀が故宮を出ると清室善後委員会は当時宮廷内の文物の点検と登録を行い、総計117万点余りあることが分かった。抗日戦争の時、貴重な文物が戦火による壊滅を避けるためめに、その一部分を後方に疎開した。抗日勝利後、小部分は北京に戻ったが、最も精華な文物計2972箱は1949年に台湾に運ばれ、残りの2211箱は南京に保管された。

　中華人民共和国成立後、故宮博物院は清宮収蔵文物を再び整理し、登録したが、その結果、計78万点余りあることが分かった。故宮博物院は国家博物館として、又、中華民族の貴重な文化遺産を収集保存し、保護する責任を背負っている。だから、購入や寄贈品の受け入れなどのルートを通じて新しく収蔵された文物は20万点余りある。このようなことから今では、北京本院の文物の総数は100万点以上である。

　故宮博物院が収蔵している文物は数量の上で驚かされるものであるだけでなく、内容と質も世界から注目されている。時代的には、遠く原始社会の新旧石器時代から、商、周、秦、漢、隋、唐、五代、両宋を経て元、明、清と現代までそれぞれに代表的な文物がある。それらの文物を系統的に展示すればまさに中華民族数千年の文化芸術の発展の歴史の縮影図となるだろう。それらの文物の類別から見れば陶磁器、玉器、青銅器、碑石、印璽、書画、漆器、琺瑯器、織繍品、金銀器、各種宝石製品、木竹牙彫、家具などがある。実に豊富多彩で立派であり、枚挙に暇がないほどである。これらのものはわが国の最も豊富な文化芸術遺産の至宝である。

　このように数量が多くて、歴史が古く、豊富多彩な文化芸術品の珍蔵を全部資料に整理し、出版して、人人に紹介することはほとんど不可能である。今度出版の『故宮珍宝』はまさに万に一を選りすぐったものであるが、私達の目的は、歴史文物を研究するのにあるのではなく、むしろ、これを通して、北京の故宮博物院には一体どのようなものが収蔵されているかということを訪れる皆様方に知ってもらい、そして、深い印象を残してもらいたいということにある。この図録に登載された収蔵品は限られているけれども、精選された芸術品が多く、また歴史の範囲が広く、代表的なものばかりであり、この目的が達せることが出来るであろう。

　中華民族は歴史の長い偉大な民族であり、尽きることのない智恵と力を持ち、豊富な想像力と創造性豊かな才能を備えて、未来への憧憬と自信に満ちている。故宮の宮殿建築とそこに収蔵されている文化芸術品の鑑賞を通して、故宮博物院に来られた観光客はどなたでもそのようなことを身に感ずるであろう。中華民族が創造した歴史文化の財産は世界人民の貴重な財産でもある。加えて故宮博物院はすでに国連ユネスコから「世界文化遺産」と指定されている。皆様の一人一人がこの文化芸術の宝庫に関心をお寄せ下さり、そして、それを愛し保護して下さることを衷心より願っている。

故宮博物院副院長　楊　新

FORWARD

The Palace Museum is world-famous not only for its magnificent buildings, which attract thousands of Chinese and foreign visitors, but also for its rich collections of cultural relics and art treasures. In order to help the vast numbers of visitors to have a better knowledge of this treasure-house of the Oriental ancient culture and art, we have compiled an illustrated book with the title of "Forbidden City", mainly to give an introduction of the architecture of the Imperial Palace; and to continue the work, now we'd like to provide this new book, "Treasures of the Imperial Palace", to give a brief introduction about its collections.

In the dynasties of past ages, imperial families used to spend great efforts to collect art works, cultural relics and rare curios, and particularly so in the Ming and Qing Dynasties. The Palace Museum, based on the Ming and Qing palaces, had inherited most of its collections. When the last Emperor Puyi was driven out of the palace in 1924, the Committee Taking Care of the Palace then made an inventory of all its collections, which amount to more than 1,170,000 pieces. During the War of Resistance against Japan, a large number of the collections were packed and transported to the rear area to avoid war damages, of which a small part was brought back to Beijing after the Japanese surrendered, but 2972 cases of the best were shipped to Taiwan in 1949 and 2211 cases of the unshipped were kept in the warehouse in Nanjing.

After the founding of the People's Republic of China, the Palace Museum once again checked and sorted out the collections of cultural relics in the Qing palace and found there remained over 780,000 pieces. As a national museum the Palace Museum also has the responsibility to collect and protect Chinese cultural relics and historical legacies, and its new collections, purchased or donated, have exceeded 200,000 pieces. Now there are more than a million pieces of various cultural relics in the Museum.

The Palacee Museum strikes people not just with the quantity of its collections, but also with the contents and quality. In accordance with the development of history, its collections involve all ages from the primitive society (including the paleolithic period and the neolithic age) throught the Shang Dynasty, Zhou Dynasty, Qin Dynasty, Han Dynasty, Sui Dynasty, Tang Dynasty, Song Dynasty, Yuan Dynasty and Ming Dynasty down to the Qing Dynasty and modern times. If the collections are exhibited chronologically, it would be an epitome of the history of several thousand years of Chinese culture. As for the categories, its collections include potery, jadewares, bronzes, steles, seals, calligraphy, paintings, lacquerwares, cloisonnes, tapestries and embroideries, gold and silver wares, articles of gems, carvings of bamboo, wood, ivory and bone, various furnitures, etc. which no doubt can be a big feast for the eyes. In fact, they are the most precious cultural legacies of our country.

For such a large quantity and variety with such a long history, it is almost impossible to illustrate all the collections to public audience. Those presented in the "Treasures of the Imperial Palace" are indeed a very small part, perhaps only one in ten thousand. However, our main purpose is not to make a study of the historical legacies but to give an initial introduction to the visitors about them so that they may have deep impressions of what are collected in the Palace Museum. It is true that the volume of this book is not big enough, but it provides a good assortment and covers a long historical period and therefore, it is typically representative of the Museum's collections and would meet our purpose.

The Chinese nation is a great nation that has a long history. The Chinese people have inexhaustible wisdoms, unlimited energies, rich imaginations and boundless creativities, and they are hopeful and confident about the future. I think all visitors to the Forbidden City would have the same opinions after they see the architecture of the Imperial Palace and the cultural treasures collected in the Palace Museum. The cultural wealth created by the Chinese nation is also a precious property of the working people of the world. The Imperial Palace has been listed by UNESCO as a cultural heritage under world protection. We wish people all over the world would love, take care of and protect this Oriental treasure-house of culture.

Yang Xin   Deputy Director of the Palace Museum

1. 三羊尊
商代後期（公元前十四世紀—前十一世紀）
高 52、口徑 41.3、腹寬 61、底徑 35.5 厘米，
重 51.2 千克。

1. 三羊尊
殷(商)時代後期(紀元前 14～11 世紀)
高 52cm 口径 41.3cm 腹幅 61cm
底径 35.5cm 重 51.2kg

1. Three-Sheep Zun（wine container）
Late Shang Dynasty(14th-11th century B.C.)
height：52 cm；diameter of mouth：41.3 cm；
width of belly：61 cm；
diameter of bottom：35.5cm；weight：51.2 kg.

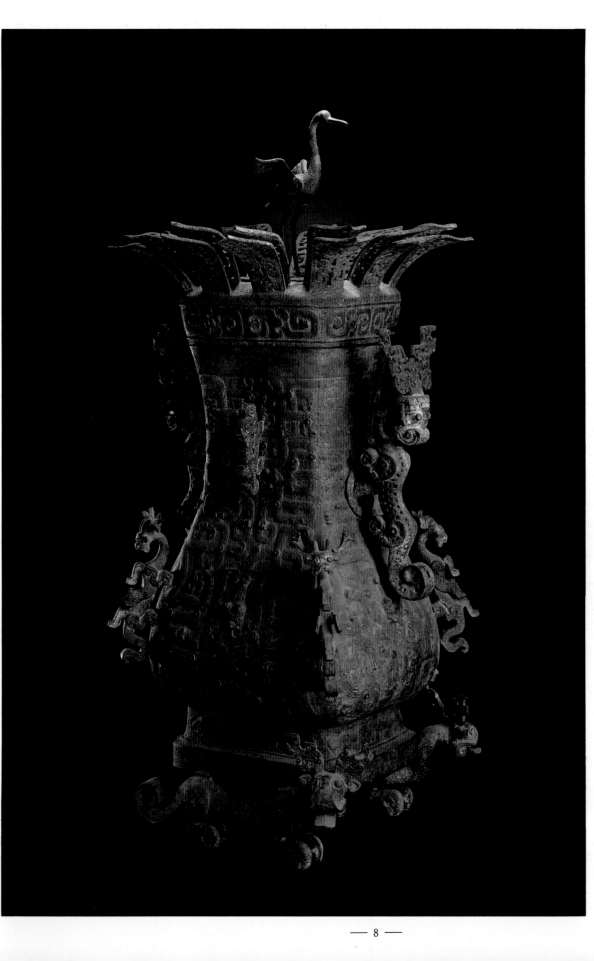

3. 立鶴方壺

春秋時期（前 770—
前 476 年）高 118、口徑
30.5 厘米，重 64.28 千克。

3. 立鶴方壺

東周（春秋）時代（紀元前
770-前 476）高 118cm 口径
30.5cm 重 64.28kg

**3. Fang Hu with Design of
Standing Crane**

Spring-Autumn Period
(770-476 B.C.)
height：118 cm；diameter
of mouth：30.05 cm；
weight：64.28 kg.

2. 鳥紋爵
西周前期（前十一世紀—前十世紀中）
高 22、流至尾長 17.7 厘米，重 1.25 千克。

2. 鳥紋爵
西周時代前期(紀元前 11—前 10 世紀)
高 22cm 口径 17.7cm 重 1.25kg

2. Jue with Bird Motif
Early Western Zhou Dynasty(11th-10th century B.C.)
height：22 cm；length(from spout to
tail)：17.7 cm；weight：1.25 kg.

4. 青玉雲紋燈
戰國
高 12.8、盤徑 10.2、足徑 5.9 厘米。

4. 青玉雲紋燈
東周(戰国)時代
高 12.8cm 盤径 10.2cm 台座径 5.9cm

4. Green Jade Lantern with Cloud Motif
Warring States Period
height：12.8 cm；diameter of plate：10.2cm；
diameter of base：5.9 cm.

5. 玉鳥紋樽
西漢
通高 12.3、口徑 6.9、足徑 6.8厘米。

5. 玉鳥紋樽
前漢時代
高 12.3cm 口径 6.9cm 足径 6.8cm

5. Jade Zun with Bird Motif
Western Han Dynasty
overall height:12.3 cm;diameter of mouth:
6.9 cm;diameter of bottom:6.8 cm.

6. 玉"長樂"穀紋璧
東漢
通高 18.6、寬 12.5、孔徑 2.6、厚 0.5厘米。

6. 玉「長楽」穀紋璧
後漢時代
高 18.6cm 幅 12.5cm 孔径 2.6cm 厚 0.5cm

6. Jade Bi with Grain Design，known as"Chang-le"
Eastern Han Dynasty
overall height:18.6 cm;width:12.5 cm;diameter
of hole:2.6 cm;thickness:0.5 cm.

7. 青釉堆塑穀倉罐
吳·永安三年
高 46.4、底徑 15.3厘米。

7. 青釉堆塑穀倉罐
呉(三国時代)永安三年
高 46.4cm 底径 15.3cm

7. Celadon Grain Jar
Third Year of Yongan Period of the Wu Kingdom
height:46.4 cm;diameter of bottom:15.3 cm.

8.《洛神賦圖》卷之一

晉·顧愷之

絹本設色。縱 27.1、橫 572.8 厘米。

8. 洛神賦図卷一

西晋時代　顧愷之

絹本著色　縱 27.1cm　橫 572.8cm

8. Painting of Luo Shen Fu(scroll)Part Ⅰ

by Gu Kaizhi , Jin Dynasty

size：27. 1 x 572. 8 cm.

painted on silk.

《洛神賦圖》卷之二

洛神賦図卷二

Painting of Luo Shen Fu(scroll)Part Ⅱ

賦本無何有圖雍色即空傳
神惟夢弱攡狀笑驚鴻子建
文中俊長康畫裏雄二難今
茲美把卷拂靈風
乾隆辛酉小春御題

《洛神賦圖》卷之三
洛神賦図卷三
Painting of Luo Shen Fu（scroll）Part Ⅲ

《洛神賦圖》卷之四
洛神賦図卷四
Painting of Luo Shen Fu（scroll）Part Ⅳ

9. 青玉鏤雕飛天珮

   唐

   長 7.1、寬 3.9、厚 0.7 厘米。

9. 青玉透雕飛天珮

   唐時代

   長 7.1cm 幅 3.9cm 厚 0.7cm

9. Green Jade Pendant with Engraved Flying Figure

   Tang Dynasty

   length：7. 1 cm；width：3. 9 cm；thickness：0. 7 cm.

10.青釉鳳頭龍柄壺
　　唐
　　高 41.3、口徑 9.3、
　　足徑 10.2 厘米。

10.青釉鳳首龍柄壺
　　唐時代
　　高 41.3cm 口径 9.3cm
　　底径 10.2cm

**10. Celadon Pot with Phoenix-head
Top and Dragon Handle**
Tang Dynasty
height: 41.3 cm; diameter of
mouth: 9.3 cm; diameter of
bottom: 10.2 cm.

11.《寫生珍禽圖》卷

　　五代・黃荃

　　絹本設色。縱 41.5、橫 70 厘米。

11. 写生珍禽図巻

　　五代　黃筌

　　絹本著色　縱 41.5cm 橫 70cm

11. Paintig：Rare Birds from Nature（scroll）

　　by Huang Quan，Five-Dynasty Period

　　size：41.5 cm x 70 cm；painted on thin，

　　tough silk.

12. 定窯孩兒枕
　宋
　高 18.3、長 30、寬 11.8 厘米。

12. 孩児枕（定窯）
　宋時代
　高 18.3cm 幅 30cm 奥行 11.8cm

12. Porcelain Pillow in the Shape of Child，
from the Ding kiln
　Song Dynasty
　height：18.3 cm；length：30 cm；
　width：11.8 cm.

13.《貨郎圖》卷

宋・李嵩

紙本淡設色。縱 25.3、橫 70.4 厘米。

13. 貨郎図卷

宋時代　李嵩

紙本淡彩　縱 25.3cm 橫 70.4cm

13. Painting：Itinerant Pedlar（scroll）

by Li Song，Song Dynasty

size：25.3 cm x 70.4 cm；painted

on paper.

14.《清明上河圖》卷之一

宋・張擇端

絹本設色。縱 24.8、橫 528 厘米。

14. 清明上河図卷一

宋時代　張擇端

絹本著色　縱 24.8cm 橫 528cm

14. Painting：Outing at the Bian River in Spring（scroll）Part Ⅰ

by Zhang Zeduan，Song Dynasty

size：24.8 cm x 528 cm.

painted on silk scroll.

《清明上河圖》卷之二　　Painting：Outing at the Bian River in
清明上河図卷二　　　　Spring（scroll）Part Ⅱ

《清明上河圖》卷之三　　Painting：Outing at the Bian River in
清明上河図卷三　　　　Spring（scroll）Part Ⅲ

15.《緙絲梅花圖》軸

　　南宋・沈子蕃

　　長 104、寬 36 厘米。

15. 緙絲梅花図軸

　　南宋時代　沈子蕃

　　縱 104cm 橫 36cm

15. **Tapestry with Pattern of Plum Blossom**

by Shen Zifan，Southern Song Dynasty

size：104 cm x 36 cm.

16. **青玉雙耳活環尊**

元

高 22.9、口徑 6.4/8.2、
足徑 6.8/9.9 厘米。

16. **青玉双耳遊環尊**

元時代

高 22.9cm 口径 6.4/8.2cm

底径 6.8/9.9cm

16. **Two-Eared Jade Zun with
Loose Rings**

Yuan Dynasty

height：22.9 cm；diameter

of mouth：6.4/8.2 cm；diameter

of bottom：6.8/9.9 cm.

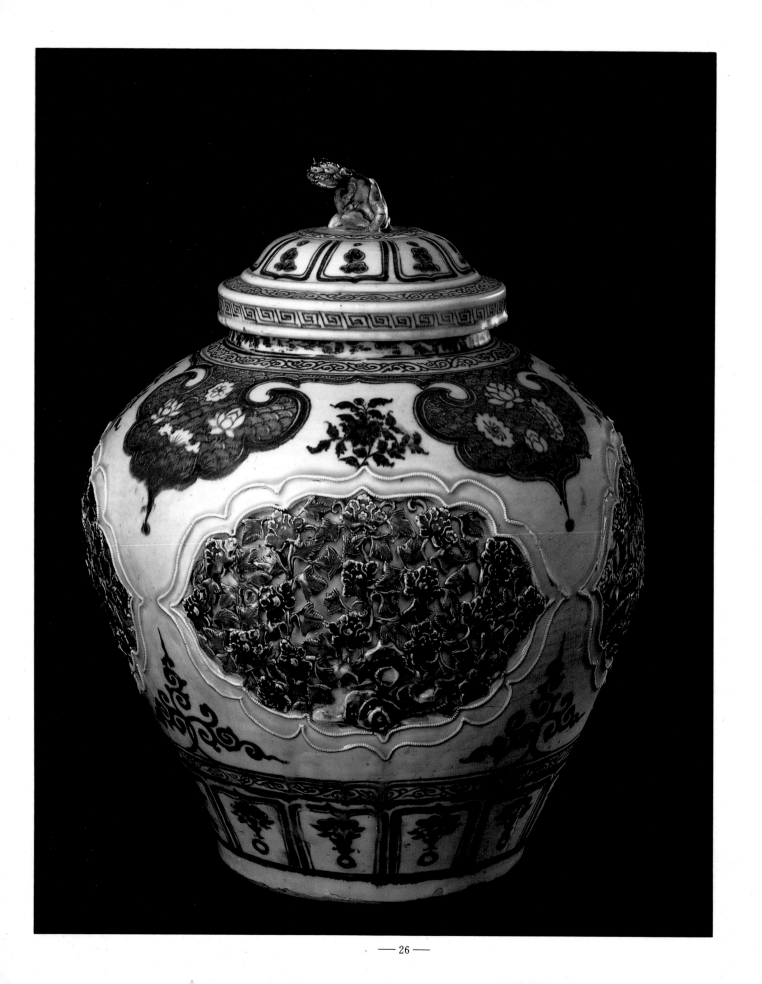

17. 青花釉裏紅開光鏤花蓋罐

元

高 41、口徑 15.5、底徑 18.5 厘米。

17. 青花釉裏紅開光鏤花蓋罐

元時代

高 41cm 口径 15.5cm 底径 18.5cm

17. Blue-and-White Covered Jar with Underglaze Red

Yuan Dynasty

height：41 cm；diameter of mouth：15.5 cm；

diameter of bottom：18.5 cm.

unearthed in May 1934 in Baoding，Hebei Province.

18. 掐絲琺瑯纏枝蓮象耳爐

明早期

通高 13.9、口徑 16、足徑 13.5 厘米。

18. 掐絲琺瑯纏枝蓮象耳炉

明時代早期

通高 13.9cm 口径 16cm 底径 13.5cm

18. Cloisonne Censer with Lotus-Scroll Design and Ears Shaped like Elephant's Head

Early Ming Dynasty

height：13.9 cm；diameter of mouth：16 cm；

diameter of bottom：13.5 cm.

19. 剔紅穿花龍雙耳瓶
   明中期
   高 36.2、口徑 4.5、足徑 10.9/9.1 厘米。

19. 堆朱穿花龍双耳瓶
   明時代中期
   高 36.2cm 口径 4.5cm 底径 10.9/9.1cm

19. Two-Eared Red Lacquered Jar with Carved
   Designs of Dragons among Flowers
   Mid-Ming Dynasty
   height：36.2 cm；diameter of mouth：4.5 cm；
   diameter of bottom：10.9/9.1 cm.

20.《王蜀宫妓圖》軸
   明·唐寅
   絹本設色。縱 12.47、橫 63.6 厘米。

20. 王蜀宫伎図軸
   明時代　唐寅
   絹本著色　縱 12.47cm 橫 63.6cm．

20. Painting：Court Ladies of Former Shu
   By Tang Yin，Ming Dynasty
   size：14.27x63.6 cm.
   painted on silk scroll.

21. 德化窰達摩立像
    明
    高 43 厘米。

21. 達磨立像（德化窯）
    明時代
    高 43cm

21. **Standing Figure of Bodhi-Dharma，**
    from the Dehua kiln
    Ming Dynasty
    height：43 cm．

22. **青花海水白龍扁瓶**
    明·宣德
    高 45.3、口徑 7.8、
    底徑 14.5 厘米 。

22. 青花海水白龍扁瓶
    明時代（宣德年間）
    高 45.3cm 口径 7.8cm
    底径 14.5cm

22. **Blue-and-White Oblate Jar with**
    Designs of Dragons in the Sea
    Xuande Period，Ming Dynasty
    height：45.3 cm；diameter
    of mouth：7.8 cm；diameter of
    bottom：14.5 cm．

23. 掐絲琺瑯勾蓮紋花觚
  明·景泰
  高 14.4、口徑 8、足徑 4.7
  厘米。

23. 掐絲琺瑯勾蓮紋花觚
  明時代(景泰年間)
  高 14.4cm 口径 8cm
  底径 4.7cm

23. Cloisonne Gu (wine container) with Designs of Lotus Scrolls
  Jingtai Period,
  Ming Dynasty
  height: 14.4cm; diameter of mouth: 8cm; diameter of bottom: 4.7 cm.

24. 鬥彩鷄缸盃
明·成化
高 3.3、口徑 8.3、底徑 4.1 厘米。

24. 鬥彩鷄甌杯
明時代（成化年間）
高 33cm 口径 8.3cm 底径 4.1cm

24. Porcelain Cup Painted with Contending Colours
Chenghua Period, Ming Dynasty
height：3. 3 cm；diameter of mouth：
8. 3cm；diameter of bottom：4. 1 cm.

25. 戧金彩漆龍鳳銀錠式盒
明·嘉靖
高 11.7、長 25.2 厘米。

25. 戧金彩漆龍鳳銀錠式盒
明時代（嘉靖年間）
高 11.7cm 幅 25.2cm

25. Painted Lacquer Box with Dragon-and-Phoenix Design Inlaid with Gold
Jiajing Period,
Ming Dynasty
height：11. 7 cm；length：
25. 2 cm.

26.**五彩魚藻紋蓋罐**
　　明·嘉靖
　　高 33.2、口徑 19.5、
　　底徑 24.1厘米。

26.**五彩魚藻紋蓋罐**
　　明時代(嘉靖年間)
　　高 33.2cm 口径 19.5cm
　　底径 24.1cm

26.**Polychrome Porcelain Covered Jar with Fish-and-Alga Design**
　Jiajing Period，Ming Dynasty
　height：33.2 cm；diameter of mouth：
　19.5cm；diameter of bottom：24.1cm.

27.**青花五彩團龍花觚**
　　明·萬曆
　　高 41、口徑 19、
　　底徑 16.6厘米。

27.**青花五彩団龍花觚**
　　明時代(万暦年間)
　　高 41cm 口径 19cm　底径
　　16.6cm

27.**Porcelain Gu with Poly-chrome Decorations**
　Wanli Period，Ming Dynasty
　height：41cm；diameter of mouth：19 cm；diameter of bottom：16.6 cm.

28. 鈿花嵌珠寶龍鳳冠
　　明·萬曆
　　高 26.5 厘米，
　　重 2.1 千克。

28. 鈿花嵌珠寶龍鳳冠
　　明時代(万曆年間)
　　高 26.5cm 重 2.1kg

28. Dragon-Phoenix Coronet
　　with Hairdress Flowers
　　Inlaid with Pearls and
　　Gems
　　Wanli Period，Ming
　　Dynasty
　　height：26.5cm； weight：
　　2.1kg 。

29. 尤通款犀角仙人槎盃
　　清初
　　高 11.7、長 27、寬 8.7 厘米。

29. 犀角仙人槎杯
　　清時代初期　尤通
　　高 11.7cm 幅 27cm 奥行 8.7cm

29. Raft-like Cup of Rhinoceros Horn with
　　Designs of Celestials
　　by You Tong，Early Qing Dynasty
　　height：11.7cm；length：27cm；width：8.7cm.

30.碧玉太平有象（一對）

　　清中期

　　高 19.7、長 25.5 厘米。

30.碧玉太平有象（一対）

　　清時代中期

　　高 19.7cm 幅 25.5cm

30. Jade Elephants（a pair）

　　Mid-Qing Dynasty

　　height：19.7 cm；length：25.5 cm.

31. 竹雕東方朔星

清中期

高 8.6、底徑 6.3/5.5 厘米。

31. 竹雕東方朔星

清時代中期

高 8.6cm 幅 6.3cm 奥行 5.5cm

31. Bamboo Carving of Dongfang Shuo

Mid-Qing Dynasty

height：8.6cm；diameter of bottom：6.3/5.5cm.

32. 竹雕提樑卣

清中期

通高 20.3、卣高 17、口徑
7.4/5.6、足徑 10/8.1 厘米。

32. 竹雕提梁卣

清時代中期

通高 20.3cm 卣高
17cm 口径 7 4cm/
5.6cm 底径 10/8.1cm

32. **Bamboo-Carved "You"**
（**ancient wine container**）
with Handle

Mid-Qing Dynasty

overall height：20. 3 cm；
height of You：17 cm；
diameter of mouth：
7. 4/5. 6 cm；diameter of
bottom：10/8. 1cm.

33. 青玉盆水仙花盆景
  清
  通高 25、盆高 6.5、
  長 15.7、寬 13.4 厘米。

33. 青玉盆水仙花盆景
  清時代
  通高 25cm 盆高 6.5cm
  幅 15.7cm 奥行 13.4

33. Potted Landscape with Narcissus in a Green Jade Pot
  Qing Dynasty
  overall height：25cm；
  height of pot：6.5cm；
  length：15.7cm；
  width：13.4 cm.

34. 銅鏨花鍍金盆翠竹盆景
清
通高 25、盆高 6 厘米。

34. 銅鏨花鍍金盆翠竹盆景
清時代
通高 25cm 盆高 6cm

34. Potted Landscape of
Green Bamboo in a
Gilded Copper Pot with
Floral Designs
Qing Dynasty
overall height：25cm；
height of pot：6 cm.

35. 銅鍍金盆紅寶石梅花盆景
清
通高 38.5、盆高 9、長 22、
寬 14.5 厘米。

35. 銅鍍金盆紅宝石梅花盆景
清時代
通高 38.5cm 盆高 9cm
幅 22cm 奥行 14.5cm

**35. Potted Landscape of Ruby
Plum Blossom in a Gilded
Copper Pot**
Qing Dynasty
overall height：38.5cm；
height of pot：9 cm；
length：22cm；
width：14.5cm.

36. 犀角鏤雕螭柄獸面紋盃
清
高 13.2、口徑 15/5.6、足徑 10.4/3.9厘米。

36. 犀角透雕螭柄獸面紋杯
清時代
高 13.2cm 口径 15/5.6cm
底径 10.4/3.9cm

36. **Rhinoceros Horn Cup with Animal Mask Design and Chi-Dragon Handle in Open-Work**
Qing Dynasty
height：13. 2cm；diameter of mouth：15/5. 6 cm；
diameter of bottom：10. 4/3. 9 cm.

37. 黃玉佛手花插
　清
　高 16.1、口徑 4.5/8.2、
　足徑 2.5/5 厘米。

37. 黄玉仏手花挿
　清時代
　高 16.1cm 口径 4.5/8.2cm
　底径 2.5/5cm

37. Topaz Flower Receptacle
　in the Shape of
　Fingered Citron
　Qing Dynasty
　height：16.1cm；diameter of
　mouth：4.5/8.2cm；
　diameter of bottom：2.5/5 cm.

38. 黃楊木雕活環鏈葫蘆
　清
　高 25.7、口徑 3.5 厘米。

38. 黄楊木雕遊環鏈葫蘆
　清時代
　高 25.7cm 口径 3.5cm

38. Carved Boxwood Gourd
　with Movable Chain of
　Rings
　Qing Dynasty
　height：25 cm；diameter of
　mouth：3.5cm.

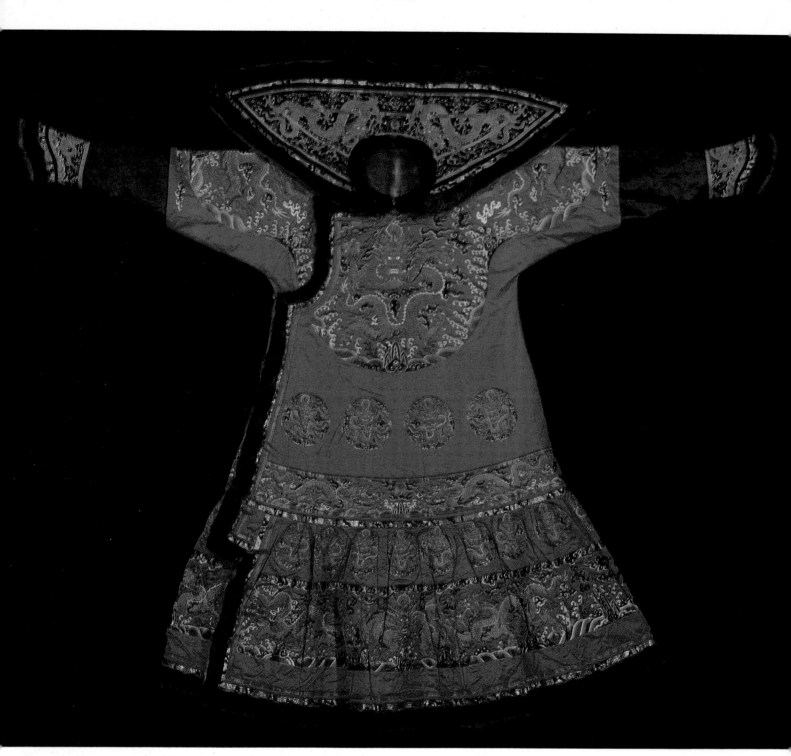

39. 明黃緞綉雲龍貂皮朝袍
  清·康熙
  身長 150、兩袖通長 204、下擺 185 厘米。

39. 明黃緞繡雲龍貂皮朝袍
  清時代(康熙年間)
  身丈 150cm 兩袖通長 204cm 裾幅 185cm

**39. Court Robe of Bright Yellow Satin with
Embroidered Patterns of Clouds and Dragons**
Kangxi Period，Qing Dynasty
length：150 cm；overall length of sleeves：
204 cm；lower hem：185 cm.

40. 畫琺瑯開光花卉瓶

清·康熙

高 13.5、口徑 4、足徑 4 厘米。

40. 画琺瑯開光花卉瓶

清時代(康熙年間)

高 13.5cm 口径 4cm 底径 4cm

**40. Painted Enamel Jar with Framed
Floral Designs**

Kangxi Period，Qing Dynasty

height：13.5cm；diameter of

mouth：4cm；diameter of bottom：4cm.

41. 琺瑯彩雉鷄牡丹盌

清·雍正

高 6.6、口徑 14.5、底徑 6 厘米。

41. 琺瑯彩雉鷄牡丹碗

清時代(雍正年間)

高 6.6cm 口径 14.5cm 底径 6cm

41. Enamel-Coloured Bowl with Design of Pheasants and Peonies

Yongzheng Period, Qing Dynasty

height: 6.6cm; diameter of mouth: 14.5 cm;

42. 石青緞綉彩雲金龍袷朝褂

清·雍正

身長 140、肩寬 40、下擺寬 124 厘米。

42. 石青緞繡彩雲金龍袷朝褂

清時代(雍正年間)

身丈 140cm 肩幅 40cm 裾幅 124cm

42. Short Court Gown of Azurite Satin Embroidered with Polychrome Clouds and Golden Dragons

Yongzheng Period, Qing Dynasty

length: 140 cm; shoulder width: 40 cm; width of lower hem: 124 cm.

43.琺瑯彩嬰戲紋雙連瓶
清·乾隆
高 21.4、口徑 5.2/9、
底徑 6/10 厘米。

43.琺瑯彩嬰戲紋双連瓶
清時代(乾隆年間)
高 21.4cm 口径 5.2/9cm
底径 6/10cm

**43. Enamel-Coloured Double-
Vase with Designs of Play-
ing Children**
Qianlong Period，Qing
Dynasty
height：21.4 cm；diameter
of mouth：5.2/9 cm；
diameter of bottom：6/10cm.

44.各色釉大瓶
清·乾隆
高 86.4、口徑 27.4、
底徑 33 厘米。

44.各色釉大瓶
清時代(乾隆年間)
高 86.4cm 口径 27.4cm
底径 33cm

44. Multicoloured Big Vase
Qianlong Period，Qing
Dynasty
height：86.4cm；diameter
of mouth：27.4 cm；diam-
eter of bottom：33cm.

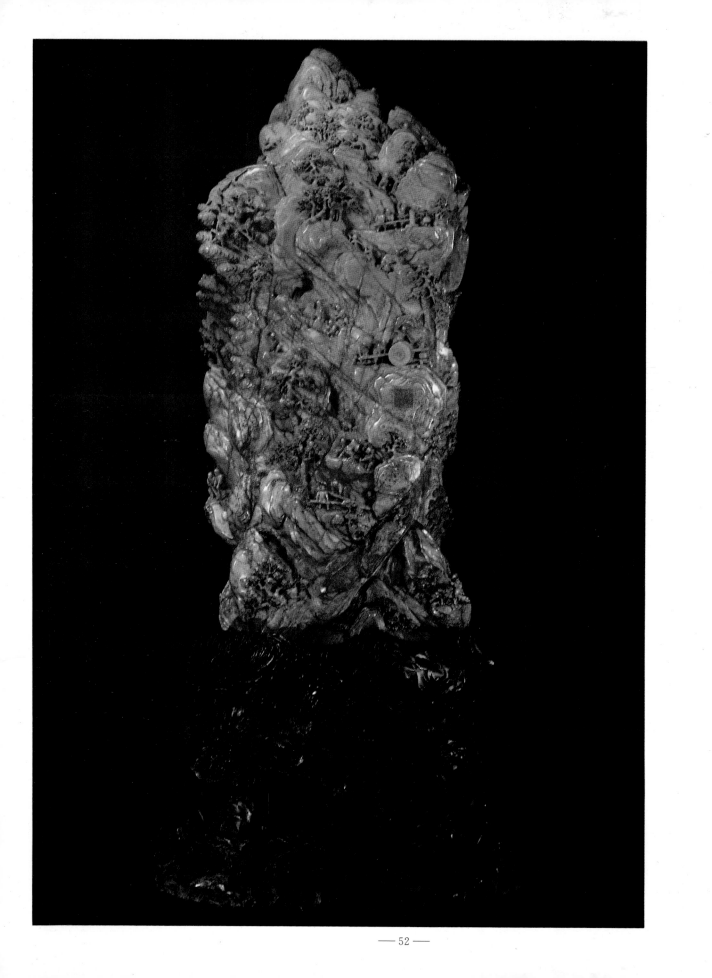

45. 大禹治水圖玉山
　　清·乾隆
　　高 240、寬 96、
　　座高 60 厘米。

45. 大禹治水図玉山
　　清時代(乾隆年間)
　　高 240cm 幅 96cm
　　座高 60cm

**45. Carved Jade Mountains
with Design of the Story
of the Great Yu(founder
of the Xia Dynasty)
Taming Waters**
Qianlong Period,Qing Dy-
nasty
height: 240cm; width:
96cm;height of pedestal:
60 cm.

46. 白玉鏤雕牡丹花薰
　　清·乾隆
　　高 7.5、口徑 13.4、足徑 8.3 厘米。

46. 白玉透雕牡丹花熏
　　清時代(乾隆年間)
　　高 7.5cm 口径 13.4cm 底径 8.3cm

**46. White Jade Censer with Peony Design in
Open-Work**
Qianlong Period，Qing Dynasty
height：7.5 cm；diameter of mouth：13.4 cm；
diameter of bottom：8.3cm.

47. 翡翠白菜式花插
　　清·乾隆
　　高 24.3、口徑 12.8/7 厘米。

47. 翡翠白菜式花插
　　清時代(乾隆年間)
　　高 24.3cm 口径 12.8/7cm

**47. Jadeite Flower-Holder in the Shape of Chinese
Cabbage**
Qianlong Period，Qing Dynasty
height：24.3cm；diameter of mouth：12.8/7cm.

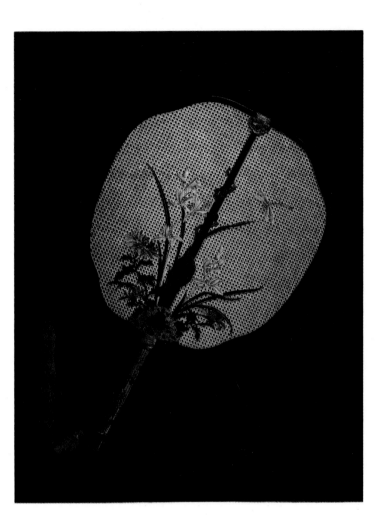

49. 象牙編織錦地蘭菊團扇
清・乾隆
通長 49.5、扇長 32.8、寬 29.9厘米。

49. 象牙編織錦地蘭菊団扇
清時代(乾隆年間)
通長 49.5cm 扇長 32.8cm 幅 29.9cm

49. **Plaited Ivory Fan**
Qianlong Period，Qing Dynasty
overall length：49.5 cm；length of
leaf：|32.8cm；|width：29.9 cm.

50. 鏨胎琺瑯犧尊
清・乾隆
高 19、身長 21.1厘米。

50. 鏨胎琺瑯犧尊
清時代(乾隆年間)
高 19cm 幅 21.1cm

50. **Champleve Zun in the Shape of Ox**
Qianlong Period，Qing Dynasty
height：19 cm；length：21.1 cm.

48. 牙雕《月曼清遊》冊（正月）
清・乾隆
縱 39.1、橫 32.9、厚 3.2厘米。

48. 牙雕「月曼清遊」冊(正月)
清時代(乾隆年間)
縱 39.1cm 橫 32.9cm 厚 3.2cm

48. **Carved Ivory Tablet of"Moonlight Amusement"**
（First Month）
Qianlong Period，Qing Dynasty
height：39.1 cm；width：32.9 cm；
thickness：3.2cm.

51. 翠"太平有象"磬
清·乾隆
高 24、長 26.5、
厚 0.7 厘米。

51. 翠「太平有象」磬
清時代(乾隆年間)
高 24cm 幅 26.5cm
厚 0.7cm

51. Jadeite Qing with Elephant Design
Qianlong Period,
Qing Dynasty
height：24cm；length：26.5
cm；thickness：0.7cm.

52. 金天球儀
清·乾隆
高 82 厘米,
重 6.071 千克。

52. 金天球儀
清時代(乾隆年間)
高 82cm 重 6.071kg

52. Gold Celestial Globe
Qianlong Period,
Qing Dynasty
height：82cm；weight：
6·071kg.

53. 織錦銅釘鐵葉盔甲
清·乾隆
上衣長 76，下裳長 71 厘米。

53. 織錦銅釘鉄葉甲冑
清時代（乾隆年間）
上衣丈 76cm 下裳丈 71cm

53. **A Suit of Armour Made of Brocade with Brass Rivets and Iron Leaves**
Qianlong Period，
Qing Dynasty
length of jacket：76cm；
length of skirt：71 cm.

54. 金嵌珠立佛像
清·乾隆
通高 54 厘米，重 19.03 千克。

54. 金嵌珠立仏像
清時代（乾隆年間）
通高 54cm 重 19.03kg

54. **Standing Buddha of Gold Inlaid with Pearls**
Qianlong Period，
Qing Dynasty
overall height：54cm；
weight：19.03kg.

55. 金佛塔
清·乾隆
高38、寬14.2厘米，
重3.45千克。

55. 金仏塔
清時代(乾隆年間)
高38cm 幅14.2cm
重3.45kg.

55. **Gold Buddhist Pagoda**
Qianlong Period，
Qing Dynasty
height：38cm；width：
14.2cm；weight：3.45kg.

56. 崇慶皇太后金髮塔
　　清·乾隆
　　高 153 厘米，重 107.5 千克。

56. 崇慶皇太后金髮塔
　　清時代(乾隆年間)
　　高 153cm 重 107.5kg

56. **Gold Pagoda for Empress
　　Dowager Chongqing**
　　Qianlong Period，
　　Qing Dynasty
　　height：153 cm；weight：
　　107.5 kg.

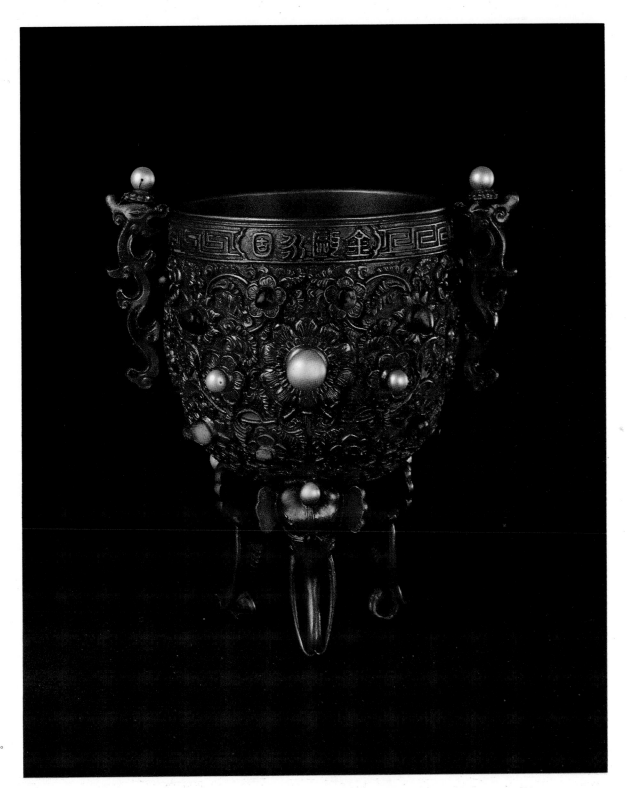

57. **畫琺瑯山水人物提樑壺**
清 · 乾隆
通高 38.1、口徑 9.1 厘米。

57. 画琺瑯山水人物提梁壺
清時代（乾隆年間）
通高 38.1cm 口径 9.1cm

57. **Painted Enamel Ewer with Handle**
Qianlong Period,
Qing Dynasty
overall height：38.1cm；diameter of mouth：9.1cm.

58. **金嵌珠"金甌永固"盃**
清 · 乾隆
高 12.5、口徑 8 厘米。

58. 金嵌珠「金甌永固」杯
清時代（乾隆年間）
高 12.5cm 口径 8cm

58. **Gold Cup Inlaid with Pearls**
Qianlong Period,
Qing Dynasty
height：12.5 cm；diameter of mouth：8 cm.

59. 白玉瓜棱提樑壺

清・嘉慶

通高 10.1、通樑高 16.8、

口徑 8.9、足徑 6.8厘米。

59. 白玉瓜棱提梁壺

清時代（嘉慶年間）

通高 10.1cm 通梁高

16.8cm　口径 8.9cm

底径 6.8cm

59. **White Jade Ewer with**
Handle，in the Shape of a
Gourd

Jiaqing Period，

Qing Dynasty

overall height：10. 1 cm；

overall height of handle：

16.8cm；diameter of

mouth：8.9 cm；diameter

of bottom：6. 8 cm.

60. 明黃緞綉彩牡丹蝶裳衣

清・光緒

身長 137.5、兩袖通長

118、袖口寬 40、下襬

寬 122 厘米。

60. 明黃緞繡彩牡丹蝶裳衣

清時代（光緒年間）

丈 137.5cm 兩袖通長

118cm 袖口幅 40cm

裾幅 122cm

60. **Bright Yellow Satin Coat**
Embroidered with
Colourful Peonies

Guangxu Period，

Qing Dynasty

length：137. 5 cm；overall

length of sleeves：118 cm；

width of cuff：40cm；

width of lower hem：

122 cm.